EVERY ANSWER IS INSIDE YOU.

START WHERE YOU ARE

meera lee patel

A TarcherPerigee Book

tarcherperigee

An imprint of Penguin Random House LLC
375 Hudson Street, New York, New York 10014

START WHERE YOU ARE

ISBN: 978-0-399-17482-7

First edition: August 2015

PRINTED IN THE UNITED STATES OF AMERICA

27

Most TarcherPerigee books are available at special quantity discounts for bulk purchases for sales promotions,
premiums, fund-raising, or educational use. Special books, or book excerpts, can also be created to fit
specific needs. For details, write: SpecialMarkets@penguinrandomhouse.com.

to you, for being exactly where you are

Introduction

It took me a long time to become comfortable with where I am.

I spent a lot of my years longing for the past or waiting for the future to arrive, confused about where I was and where I wanted to go.

Admitting to myself that I was confused and unsatisfied was difficult enough; the thought of actually doing something about it was a little too much to swallow. Instead, I welcomed distraction. I ventured down various paths for the sake of going somewhere, even though none of them took me close to where I wanted to go. I explored career paths because other people's successes made me feel like I should want them, too. I grappled. I swayed. Nothing changed; it's impossible to follow a dream that has no shape or outline.

When I realized that I couldn't continue grasping for an invisible idea, feeling, or future, I began doing some of the more difficult work that comes along with introspection. I peeled back the layers in order to find out who I really was, what was most important to me, and what it was that I wanted to cultivate in my life.

The hardest questions are the ones that open doors. Every spread in this book features a universal life lesson paired with an exercise. These exercises, often taking the form of a chart, list, or written prompt, are designed to help you apply the sentiments behind each lesson to your life. As you continue throughout the book, you'll find that some pages are harder than others – they'll ask you to dig a little deeper, face some hidden truths, or let go of ideas that you've always carried with you.

There is no right or wrong way to complete this book. If you're honest with your thoughts, these pages will serve as a mirror. You'll become privy to various pieces of yourself – some that you know very well, and others that have previously gone unnoticed.

The best advice I can give is to keep going. The process of self-discovery is just as important as any realizations that are waiting for you at the end of this book.

Take your time. Use what you have. Start where you are.

We must always be on the lookout for the Presence of wonder.

E.B. WHITE

List five things that always, and immediately, bring a smile to your face.

1 - children (babies, toddlers, elementary school kids, etc)

2 - seeing my family (mom/dads, brothers/sister, grandma, cousins)

3 - Coffee

4 - Good Music

5 - Talking about giving birth.

THERE ARE
FAR, FAR

better

things

ahead

THAN ANY WE
LEAVE BEHIND.

c.s. lewis

Write down ten big dreams that haven't come true yet.

IF YOU HAVE **GOOD THOUGHTS**, THEY WILL SHINE OUT OF YOUR FACE LIKE SUNBEAMS AND YOU WILL ALWAYS LOOK **LOVELY**.

ROALD DAHL

What are three thoughts that made you smile today?

A wise
man loses
nothing,
if he but
save himself.

MICHEL DE MONTAIGNE

Think of something you lost recently. What are two positive insights you gained from the experience?

LIVE IN THE
SUNSHINE

SWIM IN
THE SEA

DRINK THE
WILD AIR.

RALPH WALDO EMERSON

COLOR IN THIS WORLD MAP WITH THE TEN PLACES YOU PLAN TO VISIT.

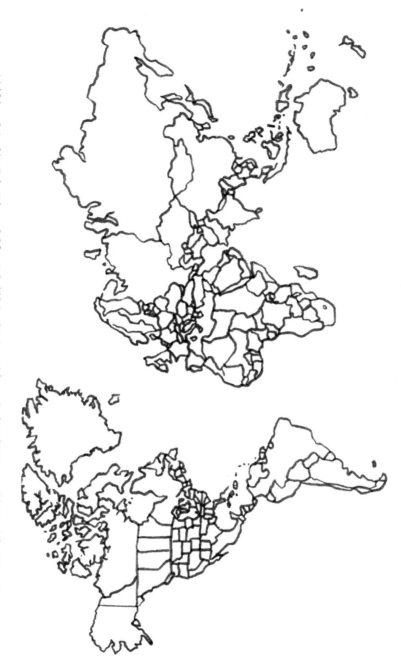

remember, you can go anywhere you like.

have a heart
that never
hardens, and
a temper that
never tires, and
a touch that
never hurts.

Charles Dickens

Write down one kind thing you did for someone else in the past 24 hours.

HAVE
PATIENCE
WITH
EVERYTHING
UNRESOLVED IN
YOUR
HEART.

Rainer Maria Rilke

- Complete lack of time due to kids being home constantly over the past 6 years, especially since last March when the coronavirus shutdown began.

- Trying to come up with energy, ideas, and motivation each day to teach & entertain my kids while simultaneously establishing a new baby's sleep, eating, etc.

- Schools being closed. Restaurants & libraries being closed, masks.

Think of something that is currently troubling you and write about it here. Don't try to solve it; just focus on getting your thoughts out of your head and onto paper.

YELLOW SPRING

HENRY DAVID THOREAU

If you could own only four possessions for the rest of your life, what would they be? Draw them here.

explore.
dream.
discover.

MARK TWAIN

DEDICATE TODAY TO LEARNING SOMETHING NEW! Describe what you learned and how this experience made you feel.

throw your DREAMS into space LIKE a kite, AND YOU do not know WHAT IT will bring back: A NEW LIFE, a new friend, A NEW LOVE, a new country.

ANAIS NIN

Write down your favorite, most daring dream on a spare piece of paper.

Fold it up and put it inside a glass bottle.

Throw it into the sea.

THE WOUND
IS THE PLACE WHERE THE
LIGHT
ENTERS YOU.

RUMI

What gives you light?

YOU GET TO DECIDE

what to

WORSHIP.

david foster wallace

CIRCLE THE THINGS YOU WORSHIP MOST.
Then underline the things you'd rather worship.

LOVE

MONEY

FRIENDSHIP

MUSIC

shoes

success

HONESTY

fame BEAUTY strength

skills

knowledge BOOKS

MEALS

CONFIDENCE

APPEARANCE talent

earth

generosity MOVIES

ADMIRATION

god

OTHER PEOPLE culture SILENCE

nature

IMAGINATION VULNERABILITY

COMPANY

solitude

pleasure laughter COMFORT

OCEAN home

DESIRE

PRIDE travel SIGHT FAMILY

fears are paper tigers.

AMELIA EARHART

Fill these tiger outlines with three of your biggest
fears, then color them in until you can't see the fear
anymore.

courage,
dear
heart

C.S. LEWIS

BREATHE IN AND OUT, DEEPLY, EIGHT TIMES.

Let your mind clear.

Move forward.

if you want to BUILD A SHIP.
don't drum up people to COLLECT WOOD.
and DON'T ASSIGN THEM tasks AND work,
BUT RATHER teach them to LONG for
the ENDLESS IMMENSITY OF THE SEA.

ANTOINE DE SAINT-EXUPÉRY

MY PASSIONS	GOALS THAT ENCOMPASS THEM

if you ever find yourself in the wrong story, leave.

mo willems

What is something you wish you could leave behind?

i have no special talents. i am only passionately curious.

ALBERT EINSTEIN

Things that excite me	Things that slow me down

IT IS NEVER TOO LATE TO BE WHAT YOU MIGHT HAVE BEEN.

GEORGE ELIOT

Things I think it's too late for	IT'S NOT TOO LATE	Step I can take to move forward
	it's not too late, it 's not too late, it's not too late, it's n ot too late, it's not	
	it's not too late, it 's not too late, it's not too late, it's n ot too late, it's not	
	it's not too late, it 's not too late, it's not too late, it's not	
	it's not too late, it 's not too late, it's not too late, it's not	

real courage is when you know you're licked before you begin, but you begin anyway and see it through, no matter what.

HARPER LEE

List four times you continued to try even though the odds were against you.

ONLY IN THE
darkness
CAN YOU SEE THE
stars.

MARTIN LUTHER KING JR.

FLIP BACK TO THE PREVIOUS PAGE.

Choose one of the difficult experiences you listed and meditate on it. Write down one lesson you've learned.

IMAGINATION
is the air of
MIND.

PHILIP JAMES BAILEY

Go outside and focus on the clouds, trees, or breeze.
Close your eyes and lift yourself out of your own
feet. Let your thoughts wander on their own.

How do you feel? Write about it here.

NO NEED TO HURRY, NO NEED TO SPARKLE, NO NEED TO BE ANYONE BUT ONE SELF.

VIRGINIA WOOLF

Things I want to be	Why I want to be them

dismiss
whatever
insults
your own
soul.

walt whitman

Think of THREE IDEAS that you fundamentally disagree with - ideas that hurt your spirit and are harmful to your well-being.

Write them down on three separate pieces of paper, and then RIP THEM UP.

the question isn't
WHO IS GOING
TO LET ME,
it's
WHO IS
GOING TO
STOP ME.

ayn rand

WHAT I WANT TO DO	WHAT OTHERS WILL THINK	WHAT OTHERS WILL DO ABOUT IT

the sun
shines not
ON us,
but IN
us.

john muir

Go outside and SQUINT AT THE SUN.

Close your eyes.

Take ten deep breaths.

AN AWAKE
HEART IS
LIKE A SKY
THAT POURS
LIGHT.

HAFIZ

Sit silently for 20 minutes; no music, conversation, reading, or writing. Take inventory of the feelings in your heart. Consider why these feelings are coming up, and write the reasons below.

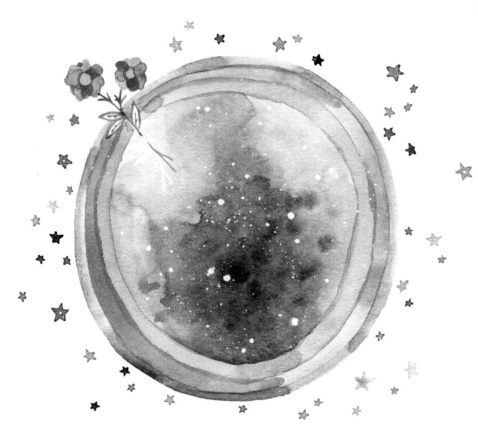

IT IS ONLY WITH THE
heart THAT ONE CAN SEE
RIGHTLY; WHAT IS *essential*
IS INVISIBLE TO THE EYE.

ANTOINE DE SAINT-EXUPÉRY

Think of an issue you've been approaching logically. Can you consider this issue through your heart's lens instead?

no one
has ever
become
poor by
giving.

ANNE FRANK

Think of something you recently gave someone.
DRAW IT HERE.

(Note: this does not have to be a tangible object.)

I'M A GREAT BELIEVER
in luck
& I FIND THE HARDER
I WORK,
the more I
have of it.

THOMAS JEFFERSON

Things I need luck for	Ways to get them without luck

live your life,
LIVE YOUR LIFE,
LIVE your LIFE.

maurice sendak

LIST YOUR SOURCES OF THE FOLLOWING:

happiness

love

courage

friendship

strength

laughter

WE ARE *one* WITH THE *wind,*
ONE WITH THE *clouds...*
ONE AS THE *waves* ARE
AT *one* WITH THE *sea!*

ALFRED NOYES

Describe something about yourself that PUSHES people away.

Now describe how it CONNECTS you.

To live is the rarest thing in the world. Most people exist, that is all.

OSCAR WILDE

COLOR IN THIS SPECTRUM WITH ALL
THE EMOTIONS YOU'VE EXPERIENCED.

anger	HURT	jealousy
joy	STRESS	frustration
EMPATHY	pride	TENSION
envy	EMBARRASSMENT	hope
DISGUST	irritation	GUILT
shame	LOVE	courage

Are there any blank areas?
Vow to experience them all.

WISDOM MEANS TO CHOOSE NOW WHAT WILL MAKE sense LATER. I AM LEARNING EVERY DAY to ALLOW THE SPACE bETWEEN where i am AND where i want to be, TO INSPIRE ME and not TERRIFY ME.

TRACEE ELLIS ROSS

GOAL	ACTION	DESIRED RESULT	ACTUAL RESULT

the only person you are destined to become is the person you decide to be.

RALPH WALDO EMERSON

List three traits you'd like others to see in you.

WE BECOME WHAT WE THINK ABOUT.

Earl Nightengale

What are your three most frequent thoughts?

What do you wish they would be?

THE ONLY JOURNEY IS THE ONE WITHIN.

RAINER MARIA RILKE

Color in each circle with the progress you've made in each area of your life.

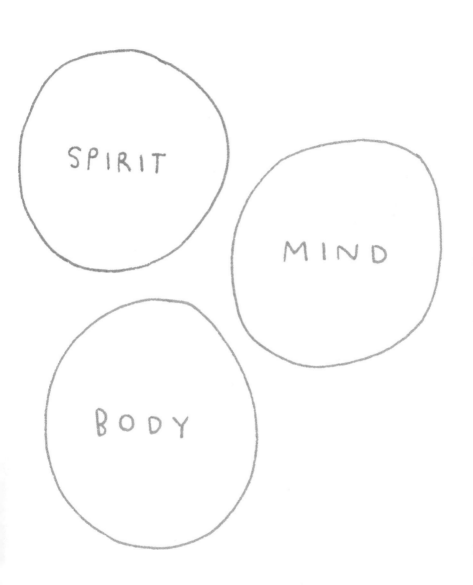

start where
you are. use
what you
have. do what
you can.

ARTHUR ASHE

Fill these shapes with resources (people, tools, ideas) that can help you on your journey.

THE BRAVE MAN
is not he who
does not
feel afraid,
but he who
CONQUERS THAT
fear.

NELSON MANDELA

DESIRE	ACTION TOWARD THAT DESIRE

Do these actions reflect courage or fear?

I AM NOT AFRAID, I WAS BORN TO DO THIS.

JOAN of ARC

WHAT IS YOUR GREATEST MOTIVATION IN LIFE?

Write it down, say it aloud, make it a part of each breath.

Now move forward.

persistence guarantees that results are inevitable.

SWAMI SMARANANANDA

Close your eyes and think about your ideal life, the one that makes you smile. Write it down on the mountain, in detail, with feeling.

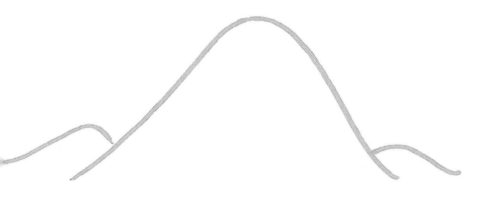

When something happens in your life that rattles you, come back to this page and remember what you most want in your life. Are your actions moving you toward the mountain?

THE WORLD
ONLY EXISTS
IN YOUR EYES.
YOU CAN MAKE
IT AS **BIG** OR AS
SMALL AS YOU WANT.

F. SCOTT FITZGERALD

Fill in each circle with what you have room for
(people, activities, feelings).

BE YOURSELF.
EVERYONE
ELSE
IS ALREADY
TAKEN.

oscar wilde

Draw a portrait of yourself using colors and patterns that reflect who you are.

WE ARE SUCH *stuff* AS
dreams ARE MADE On.

SHAKESPEARE

YOU'VE CREATED SO MANY THINGS OUT OF NOTHING.

Write about one of them here: it can be anything, like a friendship, piece of music, or new perspective.

IN THE MIDST OF
WINTER, I FOUND
THERE WAS, WITHIN
ME, AN INVINCIBLE
SUMMER.

ALBERT
CAMUS

There is always strength in the deepest of places.
Draw the source of your strength here.

i took a deep breath and listened to the old bray of my heart. i am. i am. I AM.

SYLVIA PLATH

Breathe deep and think about your place in the universe.

Think about how the particles you're made of are the same particles that make up the earth, moon, stars.

You are.

I KNEW
WHO I WAS
THIS MORNING, BUT
I'VE CHANGED
A FEW TIMES
SINCE THEN.

LEWIS CARROLL

Think of a major transformation you've been through and chronicle it here.

there is
not always
a good guy. nor
is there always
a bad guy. most
people are
somewhere
in between.

PATRICK NESS

Where do you fall on the following spectrums?

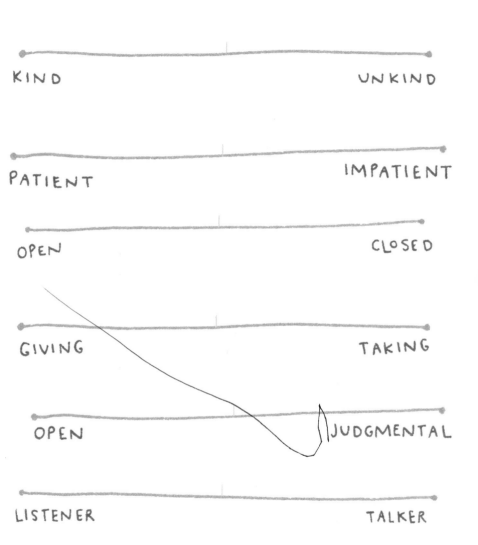

KIND ●————————————|————————————● UNKIND

PATIENT ●————————————|————————————● IMPATIENT

OPEN ●————————————|————————————● CLOSED

GIVING ●————————————|————————————● TAKING

OPEN ●————————————|————————————● JUDGMENTAL

LISTENER ●————————————|————————————● TALKER

Where would you like to fall?

it's well
we cannot hear
the screams
we make in
other people's
dreams.

EDWARD GOREY

Think about all of the people whose lives are affected by you, good or bad. Draw them here.

do you have doubts
about life? ARE YOU
UNSURE IF IT'S WORTH
THE TROUBLE?

look at the sky:
THAT IS FOR YOU.

IT'S OKAY TO BE UNSURE.

BUT praise, praise,
praise.

MIRANDA JULY

List three aspects of the human condition that you
are grateful for.

I'VE DREAMT IN
MY LIFE
DREAMS THAT
HAVE STAYED
WITH ME EVER
AFTER... AND
ALTERED THE
COLOR OF MY
MIND.

EMILY BRONTË

GO OUTSIDE AT NIGHT AND LOOK
INTO THE VASTNESS OF THE UNIVERSE.

Make a wish and write it down here:

REPEAT ONCE A MONTH, until you have a page full of
wishes that are out in the world, slowly taking shape.

vulnerability
sounds
like truth
and feels
like courage.

BRENÉ BROWN

Think of a serious problem you are facing. How can you handle it with truth and courage?

one never knows

ANTOINE DE SAINT-EXUPÉRY

THIS PAGE IS NOT BLANK.

it is filled with EVERY possibility.

IT IS YOUR FUTURE.

be silly.
BE HONEST.
be kind.

RALPH WALDO EMERSON

MOVING BACKWARD THROUGH TIME, remember yourself
as a child. What piece of advice you would give your
future self?

BE PATIENT AND TOUGH.
SOMEDAY THIS PAIN WILL
BE USEFUL TO YOU.

ovid

Writing in a stream-of-conscious style (don't censor or think about what you're writing), describe the darkest pain that visits you from time to time.

Fill this page with that pain, and then turn the page.

THERE WAS
ANOTHER LIFE
THAT I MIGHT
HAVE HAD, BUT
I AM HAVING
THIS ONE.

KAZUO ISHIGURO

Identify three parts of your life that you wish were different. Can you come up with a reason you are grateful for each?

at first glance it
may appear too
hard.
LOOK AGAIN.
always look again.

MARY ANNE RADMACHER

MY HARDEST CHALLENGE IN THE PAST YEAR	HOW I OVERCAME IT

MY BIGGEST CURRENT CHALLENGE	HOW I CAN OVERCOME IT

IT IS NOT DOWN
ON ANY MAP;
TRUE PLACES
NEVER ARE.

HERMAN MELVILLE

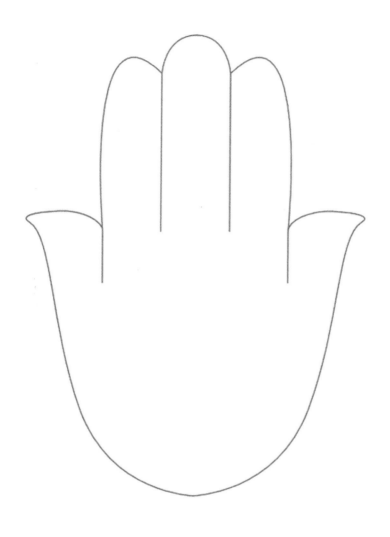

Fill in this hand to create
your own life's map.

this
above all:
to thine own self
BE TRUE.

WILLIAM
SHAKESPEARE

Close your eyes and think about what makes you feel THE MOST ALIVE.

Write it down here, and use your thoughts and actions to move closer to it all the time.

acknowledgments

My deepest gratitude to the following people who helped shape this book:

My editor, Marian Lizzi (and the entire team at Perigee), for taking a chance on me.

All of the writers, artists, thinkers, makers, and dreamers who have been my teachers in moments of need. You have given me endless inspiration and reasons to wonder and continue to help me believe that anything is possible.

My friends and family, who have always encouraged me to become the person I really am. Without you I would be lost.